Grace

A Devotion

Justin Tilghman

WESTBOW
P R E S S
A DIVISION OF THOMAS NELSON
& ZONDERVAN

WestBow Press books may be ordered through
booksellers or by contacting:

WestBow Press
A Division of Thomas Nelson & Zondervan
1663 Liberty Drive
Bloomington, IN 47403
www.westbowpress.com
1 (866) 928-1240

ISBN: 978-1-4908-2506-9 (sc)
ISBN: 978-1-4908-2505-2 (e)

Library of Congress Control Number: 2014901921

Printed in the United States of America.

WestBow Press rev. date: 02/07/2014

This small devotion is dedicated to my wife Ellen.
Without her I would have a really hard time
getting my thoughts to make sense on paper.
She is a special gift of God's grace to me.

Also, a special thanks to Jason McKnight for
your thoughtful insights and suggestions.

Thank you both for your support on this journey.

Grace

A Devotion

What is grace?

"Grace." That's a term about which we know so much and yet so little. Ask four Christians about the term and you're likely to get four different answers. It's a word that often escapes definition. Yet, it's something that is so central to our faith. We are justified by it. We are sanctified by it. And we will be glorified by it as well. It is the grace of God that elects and redeems us. It is the grace of God that sustains us. So, why is it so hard to explain? Could it be that way because the one from whom it originates is so hard to explain? This devotion will take you through many of the verses that utilize the term. The goal is not to define "grace". The goal is to describe it and show how it operates in our new lives. As you read each devotion, space is provided on the next page for you to work out your own thoughts and insights. Because, in the end, maybe it's not about defining the term but perhaps it's about understanding how it defines God and how it defines us.

What does grace mean to you? How would you define grace? How have you seen grace work in your life up until this point? Take a few moments to write out your understanding of grace as it is right now.

_____

_____

_____

_____

_____

_____

_____

_____

_____

_____

_____

_____

_____

_____

_____

_____

_____

_____

_____

_____

_____

_____

*"And the Word became flesh and dwelt among us,
and we have seen his glory, glory as of the only
Son from the Father, full of **grace** and truth"*
- John 1:14

The glory of Jesus is bound up in grace. He is the incarnate Word of God, the only begotten from the Father, and he is full of grace and truth. We often remember that Jesus claimed to be truth (John 14:6). But, how often do we think about Jesus being grace? Jesus is indeed absolute truth so is he not also absolute grace? According to this verse he is just as full of both. How might that affect our lives? When we share Jesus we often stake our lives on the hill of truth. We urge people to accept the truth of his claims as Messiah. But how might our evangelism be enhanced if we would also stake our lives just as strongly on his grace? What if we spoke just as strongly on the unmerited grace of God extended to all who might come? In the same way that Jesus is fully human and fully divine, He is also full of truth and full of grace. To offer anything less than a truthful, *and gracious*, Savior is to offer less than Jesus.

Where do you tend to focus when you share Jesus, "grace" or "truth"? How can you begin to share a more "complete" view of who Jesus is?

_____

_____

_____

_____

_____

_____

_____

_____

_____

_____

_____

_____

_____

_____

_____

_____

_____

_____

_____

_____

_____

_____

_____

_____

*"For from his fullness we have all received, **grace** upon **grace**."*
- John 1:16

We have been given an abundance of grace. That's what this verse says. And that abundance is totally founded upon the fullness of Jesus Christ. The grace of God cannot be extended to a hard, arrogant heart (James 4:6). But God has worked a miracle in that through the death of his Son He has quickened our hard, arrogant hearts. He has removed our hard, stone hearts and given us soft, humble hearts of flesh (Ezekiel 36:26). Jesus, in all His fullness of perfect obedience and humility has made it possible for God to bestow this grace upon wretched rebels such as ourselves. And He doesn't *just* bestow it but He lavishes it upon us in abundance! Jesus Himself said that He came that we might have life and have it in abundance (John 10:10). Part of that abundance is an overflow of grace in our lives. Give thanks to God that He has worked this miracle in your life because that abundant grace will be sufficient for every weakness, and strength, in your life!

Take a few moments to think on God's abundant grace. Then, right out a short prayer to God thanking Him for that grace. Be specific by sharing particular moments where His grace has been sufficient for your needs.

_____

_____

_____

_____

_____

_____

_____

_____

_____

_____

_____

_____

_____

_____

_____

_____

_____

_____

_____

_____

_____

_____

_____

*"For the law was given through Moses; **grace***
and truth came through Jesus Christ."
- John 1:17

Here it might appear that the law and grace are placed in opposition to one another. Many might be tempted to join the two phrases with "but" and argue that the law has been abolished and we are now completely under grace. While part of that is indeed true, that is not what this verse is alluding to nor is it the whole truth. Let's be careful to not take this as an opportunity to negate the law and just toss it aside in favor of grace. The law is important. The law is the backdrop for grace. But, for now, focus on this: just as God sent the law through Moses to define the lives of the Israelites, He now sends grace and truth through His Son in order to define our lives as His children. The law defined Jewish life and religious practice. Now, in the same way, grace defines those same things in the Church. So, as much as we joyfully obey God's law let us just as joyfully admire and thank Him for His grace!

It's easy to see how the law defined every day life in Israel. It was a list of do's and don'ts. But, grace is not a set of rules. So how does grace now define our lives as Christians?

_____

_____

_____

_____

_____

_____

_____

_____

_____

_____

_____

_____

_____

_____

_____

_____

_____

_____

_____

_____

_____

_____

*"...for all have sinned and fall short of the glory of God, and are justified by his **grace** as a gift through the redemption that is in Christ Jesus..."*
- Romans 3:23-24

This verse falls in the middle of a beautiful discourse on righteousness through faith in Jesus. But what does this verse say about grace? This is where we learn that it is grace that justifies us. What is justification? In short it simply means to be declared innocent and in right standing with God. So what is grace? It is that gift of God by which we are made right with Him. Did you catch that? It's a gift purchased for us by Jesus Christ. Do you do anything to earn a gift or do you simply receive it thankfully from the giver? This may seem like elementary Christianity and that's exactly what it is. This is our hope: the grace of God freely gifted to us, a rebellious creation, through the death of our beloved Savior Jesus Christ. And just as surely as everyone who falls short of God's glory has sinned and will receive just wages, so too shall everyone who trusts in the risen Savior receive this gift of grace, sufficient for total acceptance by God!

This is the scandalous side of grace. God *freely* justifies those who do not deserve His favor and only requires that they surrender their lives in acceptance of His gift. A gift comes with no strings attached, or else it wouldn't be a gift. Are you freely receiving His grace or have you imposed your own set of "requirements" in an effort to pay God back for His gift?

_____

_____

_____

_____

_____

_____

_____

_____

_____

_____

_____

_____

_____

_____

_____

_____

_____

_____

_____

_____

*"That is why it depends on faith, in order that the promise may rest on **grace** and be guaranteed to all his offspring – not only to the adherent of the law but also to the one who shares the faith of Abraham"*
- Romans 4:16

Paul is making his case that we are justified by grace through faith. Earlier in this chapter he has talked about Abraham being justified through faith. His point is that human works can never justify anyone. If our salvation were based in any part on our works, whether our choice or our good deeds, then God would not get all of the glory. Necessarily, some of the credit would rest with us. But that is not how we are saved. We are saved through child-like, dependent faith in order that our eternal life, our salvation, can wholly rest upon the good grace of God and upon that grace alone. Our salvation is meant to give God glory (Eph 1:12). Have you tried to take some of the credit for your salvation? Even as subtly as saying you chose Jesus? Maybe you think you loved God before He loved you. Understand that you love God only because He first loved you and it is solely by His grace that you chose Jesus and are saved. Give Him total credit.

God initiated the extension of grace to you. He didn't do it in response to something you did first. It was all His idea. That means grace isn't based on your performance. Do you find that relieving or does it make you uncomfortable because you want to feel like you've "earned" His grace?

_____

_____

_____

_____

_____

_____

_____

_____

_____

_____

_____

_____

_____

_____

_____

_____

_____

_____

_____

_____

_____

_____

*"Through him we have also obtained access by faith into this **grace** in which we stand, and we rejoice in hope of the glory of God."*
-Romans 5:2

We have been justified by grace through faith. That can't be said enough. The verse just before this one reiterates that point. But here we go on to see that not only are we justified by it but grace also gives us hope of seeing God in all His glory. What a sight that will be! Jesus wanted us to see that glory so badly that He prayed for it specifically in the garden (John 16:24). However, sinful humans can't see God's glory and live. Unclean souls will perish before such a holy God. So what's the answer? Something must wash those sins clean. God desired us to see His glory so much that He was willing to sacrifice His only Son in order to be able to gift us with the grace in which to stand before His throne, clean and unashamed. That's grace! Giving up His Son so that creatures that have shunned His glory might be able to look upon it. Jesus prayed for us to see His glory and God gives to us the grace needed to answer that prayer!

Again we see that grace is not fair. Why would God want to share his most precious attribute with rebels? But that is fundamental grace that God would give us something we don't deserve. How should that define the way we live, in response?

_____

_____

_____

_____

_____

_____

_____

_____

_____

_____

_____

_____

_____

_____

_____

_____

_____

_____

_____

_____

*"But the free gift is not like the trespass. For if many
died through one man's trespass, much more have
the **grace** of God and the free gift by the **grace** of
that one man Jesus Christ abounded for many."*
-Romans 5:15

Grace is not like sin. That seems like a rather obvious statement. However, what Paul is saying here is important. This is just a small piece of his discussion on the effects of the fall versus the effects of the crucifixion and resurrection. The sin of Adam brought death to the entire human race. While the effects of sin are great, the effects of grace are far greater. As Paul adds in the very next verse, death comes after only *one* transgression but the immense power of grace is shown in that, after *many* transgressions, justification comes through the grace of God. While death is the natural consequence of sin, the grace of God is powerful enough to render sin and death completely powerless! Thanks be to God that, because of Jesus Christ, such a powerful gift is freely and abundantly given!

Grace is powerful! It can undo a lifetime of sin. How have you seen that power of grace work in your life?

_____

_____

_____

_____

_____

_____

_____

_____

_____

_____

_____

_____

_____

_____

_____

_____

_____

_____

_____

_____

_____

_____

_____

_____

"For if, because of one man's trespass, death reigned
through that one man, much more will those who receive
*the abundance of **grace** and the free gift of righteousness*
reign in life through the one man Jesus Christ."
-Romans 5:17

Death is the natural byproduct of sin. Righteousness is the natural byproduct of grace. When sin entered into the world through Adam its effects were felt completely and fully. However, when grace enters the world through Jesus Christ, its effects are felt even more abundantly. Where sin has the power to kill and destroy, grace has the power to revive and renew. If you have received the grace of God and the free gift of righteousness that He offers through Jesus then you are promised, on God's word, that you will reign in this life through that grace. That means that where the effects of sin are felt the effects of grace will be felt all the more. This isn't a promise of prosperity or earthly wealth but it is a promise that, yet again, the grace of God will be abundantly sufficient for any and every need, causing you to "reign" over life's circumstances.

Has grace given you the ability to reign over life's circumstances? Take a few moments to think about that and then right specific examples where God's grace has destroyed sin's power and brought revival and renewal. Thank God for each example.

_____

_____

_____

_____

_____

_____

_____

_____

_____

_____

_____

_____

_____

_____

_____

_____

_____

_____

_____

_____

_____

*"Now the law came in to increase the trespass, but where sin increased, **grace** abounded all the more, so that, as sin reigned in death, **grace** also might reign through righteousness leading to eternal life through Jesus Christ our Lord"*
-Romans 5:20

The past few verses we have looked at have shown a common theme: grace is greater than sin. Where sin displays its power through death, grace displays its power through life. The beauty of this verse, however, is that grace is always a step ahead of sin. When sin increases, grace is there to increase all the more to bring abundant forgiveness. When death increases, grace is there to increase all the more, even unto eternal life. There is never a point where sin can outrun grace. That should comfort us. No matter where you are in your life, no matter how far you might have fallen, the grace of God, through Jesus Christ, is ever present and sufficient to forgive you, heal you, wash you, and restore you. Trying to receive grace with an unrepentant heart is to presume upon that grace. However, for the soul that humbly repents, this verse promises us that there is no amount of sin which grace cannot, and will not, defeat!

Is there an area of your life where you haven't allowed grace to overpower sin? Why not? Confess it to God. Come up with a few practical steps that will help you allow God's grace to forgive, heal, wash, or restore you in that area.

_____

_____

_____

_____

_____

_____

_____

_____

_____

_____

_____

_____

_____

_____

_____

_____

_____

_____

_____

_____

_____

_____

_____

"For sin will have no dominion over you, since
*you are not under law but under **grace**."*
-Romans 6:14

Because you are under grace, sin has no power over you. We've seen in the previous verses that grace is the antithesis of sin. Whatever sin does, grace has the power to undo. This verse takes it a step further. The Greek word for dominion here is *kyrieusei*, which means to be lord or master over something. In other words, without grace sin is our master. It controls our lives and it tells us what to do and when to do it. Also, because sin is our master we are ultimately subject to our master's wages, which is death. When we were under the law, before Christ, we only knew our sinfulness, which served to strengthen the chains of slavery we were in. However, Jesus came to bring the free gift of grace and that grace also breaks the chains of slavery to sin. Because of the grace of God, given through Jesus Christ, we are freed from the rule of sin in our lives and are now under the dominion and lordship of the most gracious being in the entire universe, Jesus Christ! Sin has lost its power. That is great news!

Where has grace broken the chains of sin in your life? Are there still chains that need to be broken?

_____

_____

_____

_____

_____

_____

_____

_____

_____

_____

_____

_____

_____

_____

_____

_____

_____

_____

_____

_____

_____

_____

_____

_____

*"For it is all for your sake, so that as **grace** extends to more and more people it may increase thanksgiving, to the glory of God"*
-2 Corinthians 4:15

As grace extends and grows to influence more people, thanksgiving increases as well. So, as we grow to understand grace more it should also lead us into more personal thanksgiving. When we truly understand what God has done for us through grace how can we not be anything but thankful? We just saw in earlier verses how grace triumphs over sin and frees us from its captivity. The purpose of grace is also wrapped up in God's glory. All things exist for him and through him and grace is no exception. As we learn to understand more and more what grace means in our own personal lives we must do our part to extend that grace into the lives of others so that they too can experience the freedom and new life that grace brings. By doing so, this verse promises that we will also be increasing God's glory, which should be the main thrust of our lives. Are you spread the glory of God's grace to lives of others?

As you grow to experience more grace and understand grace, how can you share that with someone else? Who has God placed on your heart as someone that needs His grace? What can you do today to share God's grace with them?

_____

_____

_____

_____

_____

_____

_____

_____

_____

_____

_____

_____

_____

_____

_____

_____

_____

_____

_____

_____

_____

*"We want you to know, brothers, about the **grace** of God that has been given among the churches of Macedonia, for in a severe test of affliction, their abundance of joy and their extreme poverty have overflowed in a wealth of generosity on their part"*
-2 Corinthians 8:1-2

We have talked a little about how grace is sufficient for all our needs but this verse gives us direct evidence of that. The churches in Macedonia were able to stand up under severe affliction because of the grace of God. Not only were they able to stand up under the test of affliction but also it appears that they were generously ministering to other believers. Paul mentions their poverty along side the generosity so that let's us know that they continued to give financially out of what they had. Grace makes the seemingly impossible possible. In a severe test, grace was able to provide abundant joy in the Macedonian believers through which they continued to serve the body. What about you? Have you ever experienced the abundance that God's grace provides in times of trouble? Is that experience overflowing in ministry to others? His grace is sufficient and that is a promise!

How has grace been sufficient for your troubles? Can you think of a time when God's grace enabled you to continue to serve others even in your time of trouble?

_____

_____

_____

_____

_____

_____

_____

_____

_____

_____

_____

_____

_____

_____

_____

_____

_____

_____

_____

_____

_____

_____

_____

*"For you know the **grace** of our Lord Jesus Christ, that though he was rich, yet for your sake he became poor, so that you by his poverty might become rich"*
-2 Corinthians 8:9

Grace motivated Jesus to leave the beauty and richness of heaven to come and humble himself among His creation. From this verse we learn that grace motivates us to selfless service. We are given grace to humble ourselves, so that no man can boast (1 Corinthians 1:29). Having received that grace, we should then be motivated to become "poor" for the sake of those around us who have yet to receive that grace. Then, through our humble poverty they too might become rich in grace. By poverty I mean denying one's rights and one's self. We humble ourselves and put the interests and well-being of others above our own (Romans 12:3). This is what grace and love drove Jesus to do and this is what grace should drive us to do. Are you becoming poor so that others might become rich?

Has the grace of God humbled you? How? As you grow to understand grace more, how can it drive you to humbly serve others?

_____

_____

_____

_____

_____

_____

_____

_____

_____

_____

_____

_____

_____

_____

_____

_____

_____

_____

_____

_____

_____

_____

_____

_____

_____

*"And God is able to make all **grace** abound to you,*
so that having all sufficiency in all things at all
times, you may abound in every good work."
-2 Corinthians 9:8

Again, grace is fully sufficient. If you haven't grasped that by now I hope it is beginning to sink in. This verse tells us that through grace we have absolutely everything we need at all times to do whatever good work God has set before us. Grace is the motivation and the power for good works. In true God-like fashion, He not only gives us the command to do good works (Ephesians 2:10) but He also gives us what we need to fulfill the command. Grace is what we should rely on to do good works. Are you feeling inadequate in regards to your witness? Grace should motivate you by reminding you of the wonderful gift that God has given you and then pushing you to share with others. Are you having difficulty finding motivation to serve others? Grace reminds us of how Jesus ultimately served us on the cross, thereby compelling us to serve others. So remember that the grace of God is the motivation and the power that you need to go forth and serve!

By now we have seen that grace is not just for us. Grace is a gift that must be shared. How can the grace you have been show empower you to grow in obedience as well as go out and share with those around you?

_____

_____

_____

_____

_____

_____

_____

_____

_____

_____

_____

_____

_____

_____

_____

_____

_____

_____

_____

_____

_____

_____

_____

*"But he said to me, 'My **grace** is sufficient for you,*
for my power is made perfect in weakness.' Therefore
I will boast are the more gladly of my weaknesses,
so that the power of Christ may rest upon me."
-2 Corinthians 12:9

This is probably one of the most well known verses regarding grace. Paul has asked the Lord to remove from him a thorn in his flesh. But the Lord's answer was "no" and this was His response. God's grace is the strength we need in our weaknesses. It is not just strength but rather it is all-sufficient strength. The Greek word that is translated sufficient is *arkei* and it conveys the meaning of completely sufficient for defense or standing against some thing. When sickness, poverty, trial, or temptation comes His grace is completely able to sustain us and make us stand during those times. Grace is a powerful means of defense. It is "the power of Christ" to stand against the trials of this life. How have you seen this truth played out in your life? Is there a trial you are facing in which you need to be reminded that the grace of God is a sufficient defense for you in every area of need?

Where do you need the defense of grace in your life? Where is the enemy being a "thorn in your side"? Ask God for His grace to defend you in your time of need.

_____

_____

_____

_____

_____

_____

_____

_____

_____

_____

_____

_____

_____

_____

_____

_____

_____

_____

_____

_____

_____

_____

_____

_____

*"You are severed from Christ, you who would be
justified by the law; you have fallen from **grace**."*
-Galatians 5:4

This can be a troubling verse for some. Some have argued that this means that believers can fall away from grace, never to return. There are several verses that argue against that (John 10:29, John 6:37, Heb. 13:5, etc.) so what exactly is Paul saying? In the context of Galatians as a whole, Paul is encouraging the Galatians to hold fast to the gospel of grace that was preached to them in the beginning. They are being tempted to move away from that gospel to another gospel of works and outward ritual, the law. As we just saw in the last verse, grace is our defense in time of need, especially against God's wrath. It is the power of Christ to save us. So what this verse is saying is that if you choose to find your defense in something other than Christ, you lose the defense of God's grace in all areas of life. How often are we tempted to do that? Are you looking for defense in yourself or Jesus? Confess that to God and cling today to the power of Christ that is the grace of God.

Is there any are in your life where you trust more in yourself and your abilities than in Jesus to see you through? Ask God to bring to mind specific areas. Write them down, confess them, and pray for the wisdom to release them to Jesus. Then, relax in God's grace.

_____

_____

_____

_____

_____

_____

_____

_____

_____

_____

_____

_____

_____

_____

_____

_____

_____

_____

_____

_____

_____

_____

_____

*"In him we have redemption through his blood, the forgiveness of our trespasses, according to the riches of his **grace**, which he lavished upon us, in all wisdom and insight making known to us the mystery of his will, according to his purpose, which he set forth in Christ as a plan for the fullness of time, to unite all things in him, things in heaven and things on earth"*
-Ephesians 1:7-10

Grace has so many functions. It is the source from which our forgiveness flows. It ordained the death of Jesus in order to purchase that forgiveness. It also makes known to us the will of God as purposed in Jesus. The plan of God is wrapped up in His grace. Your salvation was not an afterthought. Our sin did not sneak up on God. Our rebellion did not initiate a "Plan B" which required Jesus to die. God determined to send Jesus before the foundation of the world (Eph. 1:4, 1 Peter 1:20). Don't think he saved you because He felt like He had to. He saved you out of His rich grace. He saved you because, simply, that's who He is, a God of grace and mercy! How can you apply that truth to your life right now?

Praise God, our salvation was part of His plan! He wanted you! Think about that and then write a prayer of praise to God for his initiative of grace that determined to make a way for us before we were even born.

_____

_____

_____

_____

_____

_____

_____

_____

_____

_____

_____

_____

_____

_____

_____

_____

_____

_____

_____

_____

_____

_____

*"But God, being rich in mercy, because of the great
love with which he loved us, even when we were
dead in our trespasses, made us alive together
with Christ – by **grace** you have been saved"*
-Ephesians 2:4-5

What a comforting verse. God is "rich in mercy". The Greek term for rich used here denotes a vast abundance. God's mercy is virtually inexhaustible. His mercy is also directly linked to His love for us. But the overriding truth in this verse is that we were saved when we were least desirable. We were saved at the very moment that it seemed like we were most undeserving. That means that God chose to save you, and save me, solely because He wanted to. It pleased Him to do it. He loved us so much that He desired to make us alive with Christ so that we might spend eternity in His presence, adopted into His family, even when we were as good a dead to Him in terms of our rebellious attitude. Thanks be to God for His abundance of love, mercy, and grace! May we never cease to thank Him for the great kindness He has shown to us.

You can't exhaust God's grace. No amount of sin and failure is more than His grace can cover as long as you humbly seek His forgiveness. If you need to confess something to God, do it here all the while knowing that He graciously longs to forgive you. Otherwise, write a prayer of thanks to God for loving you even while you least deserved it.

_____

_____

_____

_____

_____

_____

_____

_____

_____

_____

_____

_____

_____

_____

_____

_____

_____

_____

_____

_____

_____

_____

*"...and raised us up with him and seated us with him in the heavenly places in Christ Jesus, so that in the coming ages he might show the immeasurable riches of his **grace** in kindness toward us in Christ Jesus"*
-Ephesians 2:6-7

The previous verse told us that it is by grace that we have been saved. We have also seen that grace is a very present reality in our lives that gives us the defense we need to stand up under trials and temptations. Now this verse tells us that all of what we have seen so far is just the tip of the iceberg! God has so much more to show us! Grace goes so much deeper than what we could ever imagine. In other words, God saved us by His grace and gives us grace to live in order that He might show us the unimaginable depths of His grace in the future through things such as continued forgiveness and our growing in Christ-likeness. By growing in Christ-likeness I mean shaping us to be satisfied in all that He is for us in Jesus. This verse demonstrates the kind heart of our Creator. Grace was active in the past to save us, is actively now saving us, and is also yet to be revealed even more in our lives through our Savior, Jesus! We haven't even begun to scratch the surface of God's kindness!

Think back to all the ways you've seen God's grace work in your life. Let's do a quick inventory. List as many ways as you can in which God has shown you His grace up until this point. Now imagine that is only the beginning. God has all of eternity to show you so much more!

_____

_____

_____

_____

_____

_____

_____

_____

_____

_____

_____

_____

_____

_____

_____

_____

_____

_____

_____

_____

_____

_____

_____

_____

*"For by **grace** you have been saved through faith.
And this is not your own doing; it is the gift of God,
not a result of works, so that no one may boast"*
-Ephesians 2:8-9

This is another very famous and often quoted verse regarding grace. The Protestant Reformation used this as one of the corner stones of the movement. We are not saved by anything that we have done. We are saved solely because of the grace and kindness of God. This grace is gifted to us through faith in Jesus. But what this verse is also saying is that both the grace that saves us *and* the faith that initiates our justification are gifts from God. Therefore we have absolutely nothing we can boast in. God initiates and completes every aspect of our salvation. The grace by which He saved us is a gift. The faith that receives that grace is also a gift. It's all from God. In this way God gets all of the glory for everything: our justification, our sanctification, and our glorification. Thank God that He loved us all enough to do everything we could not in order to effectively bring salvation into our lives.

There really was, and is, no way you could ever come to God unless He came to you. In Jesus, He has spanned the immense gap between the two of you. If you're looking for true love, that's it. Take a few moments to just thank God for who He is.

_____

_____

_____

_____

_____

_____

_____

_____

_____

_____

_____

_____

_____

_____

_____

_____

_____

_____

_____

_____

_____

_____

_____

*"Now may our Lord Jesus Christ himself, and God our Father, who loved us and gave us eternal comfort and good hope through **grace**, comfort your hearts and establish them in every good work and word"*
-2 Thessalonians 2:16-17

Grace is the vehicle by which we receive eternal comfort and good hope. In other words our hope of eternal life is as secure as the grace of God is inexhaustible and we've seen already how deep God's grace goes! But not only is grace a means of eternal comfort and hope in things yet to come but these verses also tell us that grace is effective today, in this very moment. Paul is telling the church at Thessalonica to take the grace that gives them future hope and allow it to comfort them in their everyday lives as well. That's the thought that is conveyed by "every good work and word." I don't think God wants grace to just be something that helps us to remain focused on what is yet to come. Instead grace should be something that we rest upon daily for comfort in times of trouble and support for daily obedience to do the good works that God has set before us to do.

God's grace promises you eternal life with Him in heaven. How does that promise of future blessing give you strength to live in obedience as you face the trials and temptations of today?

_____

_____

_____

_____

_____

_____

_____

_____

_____

_____

_____

_____

_____

_____

_____

_____

_____

_____

_____

_____

_____

_____

*"You then, my child, be strengthened by the **grace**
that is in Christ Jesus, and what you have heard from
me in the presence of many witnesses entrust to
faithful men who will be able to teach others also."*
-2 Timothy 2:1-2

Paul is telling Timothy to allow God's grace to strengthen him. We have seen several times already how grace is a means of strength in the Christian life. We saw earlier that grace is a means of enduring in weakness. Here we see that grace is a catalyst for the continuation of the church. Paul is specifically talking to Timothy regarding the selection of church leaders who will be able to pass on sound doctrine. That will be difficult. So, in order to do that Timothy must be strengthened by the grace that is available to him in Jesus. That grace will empower him and guide him to make the right decisions. What does that mean for us? How often do we only lean on God's grace in moments of weakness? According to this verse we should lean on God's grace not only in weakness but in times of obedience and making disciples as well. We're beginning to see that God's grace permeates every corner of the Christian's life: from weaknesses to strengths, from temptations to obedience, from our own lives to the sharing of the gospel in other's lives as well.

If God's grace is meant to help us in all areas of life and not just in weakness, in what areas do you need to begin to rely more on God's grace?

_____

_____

_____

_____

_____

_____

_____

_____

_____

_____

_____

_____

_____

_____

_____

_____

_____

_____

_____

_____

_____

_____

_____

_____

*"For the **grace** of God has appeared,*
bringing salvation for all people,"
- Titus 2:11

What a powerful verse. Out of all the things we have seen about God's grace thus far, this is by far the greatest. The grace of God has brought us salvation! That means it also brings about everything needed for salvation. Through the Holy Spirit, God's grace opens up our eyes to see the glory of God in the face of Jesus (2 Cor. 4:4). God's grace woos our hearts and minds and turns our affections toward Jesus. God's grace enables us to confess our sins and place our faith in Jesus as our only Lord and hope for salvation (1 Cor.12:3). God's grace enables us to persevere in faith so that we will be able to stand before the Son of Man on the last day (Luke 21:36). God's grace enables us to die to ourselves daily and live in abandon to the good works that God has prepared in advance for us to do (Ephesians 2:10). Praise God for His grace that was demonstrated to us in Jesus and is applied to us through the Holy Spirit so that we might enjoy the riches of grace in salvation!

Think back on your salvation journey. Identify where God's grace was at work at each and every point to bring you to the point of saving knowledge and trust in Jesus.

_____

_____

_____

_____

_____

_____

_____

_____

_____

_____

_____

_____

_____

_____

_____

_____

_____

_____

_____

_____

_____

_____

_____

*"But when the goodness and loving kindness of God our Savior appeared, he saved us, not because of works done by us in righteousness, but according to his own mercy, ... so that being justified by his **grace** we might become heirs according to the hope of eternal life"*
-Titus 3:4-7

This concept cannot be stressed enough: we are saved because of God's goodness and kindness, not by our own works. The grace of God is completely intertwined with His goodness, kindness, love, and mercy. In other words, it is simply what He is. He justifies us solely because He is a God who graciously delights in justifying sinners. But not only does His grace justify us but it goes far beyond that. It makes us heirs! God could easily have said, "You are forgiven, now be on your way." But He doesn't. Instead He says to His enemies, "You are forgiven and now what is mine is yours." That is a level of grace that many of us can only imagine. Have we ever been that gracious? Sure we forgive others but have we then been so gracious to them as to consider them a welcomed friend or as close as family? God does it for us. And how glad I am that He does!

Again we see the scandalous nature of the grace of God. He goes far beyond what is "fair" and lavishes his former enemies with blessings. You who were once an enemy of God, destined for torment, are now a welcomed child and heir to all that He has. Think on that and then let the words of gratitude from your heart spill onto the page.

_____

_____

_____

_____

_____

_____

_____

_____

_____

_____

_____

_____

_____

_____

_____

_____

_____

_____

_____

_____

*"But we see him who for a little while was made lower than the angels, namely Jesus, crowned with glory and honor because of the suffering of death, so that by the **grace** of God he might taste death for everyone"*
-Hebrews 2:9

It was grace that brought Jesus down to us. It was grace that caused Jesus to taste death on our behalf. Grace caused the King of Glory to, for a moment, make Himself lower than His own creation so that He might redeem them from their misery. If that doesn't sum up what it means to graciously love someone then I don't think we will ever be able to explain what that means. The grace of God is the fuel for selfless, loving service. We have been shown immeasurably selfless love from Jesus by the grace of God. How are we, in turn, demonstrating that same love to the lost? By the grace of God, do we taste death for others? Not death in the sense of Jesus' sacrificial death but rather death in the sense of dying to our selves daily so that others might experience what it means to be loved by their Creator. How can you, by the grace of God, taste death for the sake of others just as Christ tasted death for your sake?

Because grace is the fuel for self-sacrifice, how can you die to yourself for the sake of others today, this week, this year? Be specific.

_____

_____

_____

_____

_____

_____

_____

_____

_____

_____

_____

_____

_____

_____

_____

_____

_____

_____

_____

_____

_____

_____

_____

_____

*"Let us then with confidence draw near to the throne of **grace**, that we may receive mercy and find **grace** to help in time of need."*
-Hebrews 4:16

What a great verse. We who were once enemies of God, destined to be forever banished from His presence can now, because of the grace of God demonstrated to us through Jesus, confidently draw near to His very throne in time of need. Read that sentence again and let that truth sink in. In our sin we were destined for wrath. But the grace of God is so extremely powerful, deep, and far-reaching that we are now not only allowed into His presence, we are told to approach confidently! It's hard to really explain how strong of a confidence is conveyed by the Greek term used for "confidence" in this verse. God's grace allows us to approach Him unashamed of our past, boldly, and with full and complete assurance of His care, just as we would approach our greatest friend or most loving parent here on earth if we had a need. God longs to give you more grace and mercy as you have need. Confidently ask Him for it today and be assured that He will indeed give you what you need.

Have you been afraid to approach God? Do you feel unworthy? His grace encourages you to come to Him. He is a faithful friend and loving father. Because of Jesus you are accepted and welcomed to the very throne room. As we knock on the door to the throne, I can almost hear His voice now, "Come in my little one, I have been waiting for you!" Talk to Him.

_____

_____

_____

_____

_____

_____

_____

_____

_____

_____

_____

_____

_____

_____

_____

_____

_____

_____

_____

_____

_____

*"Concerning this salvation, the prophets who prophesied
about the **grace** that was to be yours searched and
inquired carefully, inquiring what person or time the
Spirit of Christ in them was indicating when he predicted
the sufferings of Christ and the subsequent glories"*
-1 Peter 1:10-11

Many people believe that grace is something that was introduced to us in the New Testament. Some argue that the God of the Old Testament is different from the God of the New Testament. But this verse shows just the opposite. Grace has always been at the heart of who God is. The prophets of the Old Testament knew that and earnestly awaited Messiah's arrival because they knew that it would be the physical manifestation of God's grace to humanity. Don't think that grace through Jesus was an afterthought. Grace had been experienced in the Old Testament (God forgiving Abraham's lack of trust, Moses' anger, David's adultery, etc.) but Jesus' arrival would bring about an unprecedented outpouring of God's grace. Praise God that we have the honor and the privilege of being on this side of Jesus' arrival.

Grace is not just a New Testament concept. Can you think of other ways that grace was experience in the Old Testament? As you write them here, begin to realize that graciousness has *always* been a part of God's character.

_____

_____

_____

_____

_____

_____

_____

_____

_____

_____

_____

_____

_____

_____

_____

_____

_____

_____

_____

_____

_____

_____

_____

*"Therefore, preparing your minds for action, and being sober-minded, set your hope fully on the **grace** that will be brought to you at the revelation of Jesus Christ"*
-1 Peter 1:13

Grace is not only a present reality. It is also a future concept as well. John Piper refers to this concept as, simply, "future grace."[1] Grace saves us in the present but it does not allow us to stay stagnant. The idea of future grace empowers us to "prepare our minds for action" and live lives of obedience. Much like the parable of the talents in Matthew 25, we have been given present grace as a gift to be invested in light of future grace. As the servants in that parable were given gifts and talents, we are given grace, and grace upon grace (John 1:16), so that we might invest in the Kingdom and further God's glory. But why do we do these things? We do them because we are hopeful of future grace that God will show us when Jesus returns. In other words, God's grace is not something that we receive and keep to ourselves. God's grace compels us to be action oriented in hope of future grace. How are you doing in regards to the hope of future grace?

---

[1]   John Piper, *Future Grace: The Purifying Power of the Promises of God*, (Colorado Springs: Multnomah Books, 1995)

Are there areas where you could be more obedient? Are there areas where you could be more forgiving? Are there sins that you struggle with? How can hope of future grace help you in those areas?

_____

_____

_____

_____

_____

_____

_____

_____

_____

_____

_____

_____

_____

_____

_____

_____

_____

_____

_____

_____

_____

_____

*"As each has received a gift, use it to serve one
another, as good stewards of God's varied **grace**"*
-1 Peter 4:10

Grace should be shared. It is not given to us so that we might keep it to ourselves. Grace is given to us so that we might be enabled to serve one another. The term "steward" in this verse carries the idea of a manager of an estate. We have been given a measure of God's grace to manage. That grace is a gift to be shared with the body of Christ. You might have been graced with the gift of encouragement, encourage the body. You might have been graced with the gift of helps, serve those in need. You might have been graced with the gift of teaching, help others to understand the Word. Whatever gift of grace you have been given, find ways to share it with the body. What are you good at? Where are your talented? What brings you joy? What things have others said you are good at? What do people often ask you to do or seek your help in? List your gifts on the next page and ask God to identify some ways you can serve someone else with that gift with which He has graced you.

Gift	Ways to use this gift
_____	_____
_____	_____
_____	_____
_____	_____
_____	_____
_____	_____
_____	_____
_____	_____
_____	_____
_____	_____
_____	_____
_____	_____
_____	_____
_____	_____
_____	_____
_____	_____
_____	_____
_____	_____
_____	_____
_____	_____
_____	_____
_____	_____
_____	_____
_____	_____

"Clothe yourselves, all of you, with humility toward one another,
*for 'God opposes the proud but gives **grace** to the humble'"*
-1 Peter 5:5b

There has been much said about grace so far. We have seen that grace is a past gift, a present reality, and a future hope. We have seen that grace saves us, sustains us, and ultimately glorifies us. Now this verse illustrates the recipients of grace. If you want more grace in your life, come in a spirit of humility. Come knowing that you don't deserve any measure that God chooses to give to you. Come realizing that without this gift you will not survive. Not only must you come to God with a humble spirit but you must also demonstrate humility toward your fellow believer. Grace is only given to those who humbly seek it. Can you think of some areas where you could demonstrate more humility toward God? Are there areas where your pride is keeping you from receiving the grace you need? Can you think of individuals toward whom you could be more humble? Ask God to create in you a humble spirit that is ready to receive the grace He has to offer you.

List some areas where you struggle with humility. Where is pride keeping you from receiving grace? Who can you show grace to today, this week, and this year? Ask God to help you answer these questions.

_____

_____

_____

_____

_____

_____

_____

_____

_____

_____

_____

_____

_____

_____

_____

_____

_____

_____

_____

_____

_____

_____

_____

_____

_____

*"But grow in the **grace** and knowledge of
our Lord and Savior Jesus Christ"*
-2 Peter 3:18

Grace. What a precious gift. What a strong reality. We've explored in depth what grace is. It is something that has been given to us. It is something that we presently rely on daily. It is something that we long and hope for in the future. However, we've barely even scratched the surface of what grace is and what it means in our lives. The challenge now is to continue to grow deeper. Continue to plumb the depths of what God's grace means in your life and in our lives as the body of Christ. If we make it our goal to continue to grow in the grace and knowledge of Jesus Peter tells us, in verse 17, that we will be able to stand firm in what we believe and stand firm in the faith we profess. Think of some practical ways you can grow in the grace and knowledge of Jesus and list them on the next page. Now develop a plan to implement what you wrote.

Ways you can grow in the grace and knowledge of Jesus:

_____

_____

_____

_____

_____

_____

_____

_____

_____

_____

_____

How will you accomplish these things?

_____

_____

_____

_____

_____

_____

_____

_____

_____

_____

_____

_____

Defining grace

Well we've reached the end of our journey. I hope you've gained a deeper understanding of what grace is. We have, in no way, exhausted the subject. To say we have only scratched the surface is an extreme understatement. I encourage you to use this small devotion as a springboard to explore more of what God's grace means. God's grace is essential to your daily life as a believer. It is because of grace that you are a believer. It is by God's grace that you remain a believer. And, it is by God's grace that each of us will enter into that eternal rest that He has prepared for those that love Him. God's grace empowers us to serve others. God's grace supports and defends us in temptations and trials. God's grace is completely sufficient for each and every need in our lives. God's grace is not solely for our benefit but rather it is a gift to be shared. I hope you have found renewed rest and comfort in God's grace. I also pray that you've found a renewed sense of dependence on God to carry you through every aspect of life. God is glorified when we rely upon His grace in our lives. Let Him pour His grace into your life today! Now, may "the grace of the Lord Jesus Christ and the love of God and the fellowship of the Holy Spirit be with you all" (2 Cor. 13:14)

Think back to what you wrote at the beginning of this devotion in regards to what grace means to you. How has your view changed over the past 31 days? How has it been challenged? How has it been strengthened?

_____

_____

_____

_____

_____

_____

_____

_____

_____

_____

_____

_____

_____

_____

_____

_____

_____

_____

_____

_____

_____

_____

_____

_____

Alphabetical Scripture Index

Notes

Notes

Notes

Notes

GRACE
OVERFLOWS
COUNSEL · DISCIPLE · CONNECT

If you've enjoyed this devotion or would like to know more about our ministry, feel free to contact us.

You can write to us at:

Grace Overflows
PO Box 5708
Kinston, NC 28503

Or visit us online at:
www.graceoverflows.org

Online, you can find more articles and resources to help you in your daily walk.

Grace and Peace to You!